ROBERT E. LEE

*Commemorative Essays on the
Bicentennial of His Birth*

ROBERT E. LEE

*Commemorative Essays on the
Bicentennial of His Birth*

The Robert E. Lee
Memorial Association

2007

All images used in this book are from the Stratford collection.

First edition

ISBN-10: 0-9790428-0-1 (hard cover)
ISBN-13: 978-0-9790428-0-5 (hard cover)

Printed in the United States

Published by The Robert E. Lee Memorial Association, Inc.
Stratford
483 Great House Road
Stratford, VA 22558
Phone: (804) 493–8038
www.stratfordhall.org

Produced by the Coventry Group, LLC, Chicago
Designed by Bockos Design, Inc., Chicago

◄•••►

Frontispiece: *Taken in early 1863, this is Robert E. Lee's first full-length portrait
as the commander of the Army of Northern Virginia.*

IN MEMORY OF
BLEECKER BURNETT ISHAM

A devoted friend to Stratford
President 1985–1988
Illinois Director 1975–1992

————◆◆◆————

CONTENTS

PREFACE

January 19, 2007, will mark the 200th anniversary of Robert E. Lee's birth here at Stratford—an important occasion to reflect upon Lee's role in American history. In honor of this occasion, and as part of an extensive celebration at Stratford, the Robert E. Lee Memorial Association is pleased to offer this volume of essays by some of our nation's most distinguished Civil War scholars.

Each of the experts who has contributed to this volume participated in the 2006 *Path of Honor* lecture series here at Stratford. We are grateful to the Lee–Jackson Educational Foundation for providing the funds that made the series possible.

We learned from these lectures that Lee's legacy will continue to inspire revision and debate. It is our hope that this small volume will serve as a tool to encourage this kind of scholarly inquiry and to re-examine one of the central figures of our nation's history as well as his remarkable family. We hope that you will keep this book and consult it often.

We also hope that this publication will encourage people to come and explore Stratford, one of America's great historic sites. In addition to being the birthplace of Lee, Stratford's 1738 Great House was also home to Richard Henry Lee and Francis Lightfoot Lee, the only brothers to sign the Declaration of Independence. Our 1,900 acres and two miles of spectacular Potomac River waterfront offer many opportunities for exploration and recreation.

Many thanks are due to Kenneth M. McFarland, director of preservation and education, and Judith S. Hynson, director of research and collections, for their work on the *Path of Honor* lecture series and their dedication to this book.

Finally, we offer thanks and gratitude to Nancy and Rob Isham for their generosity and commitment in making this volume possible, and to the Board of Directors for its support of this project and the Lee bicentennial celebration.

Paul C. Reber
Executive Director
Robert E. Lee Memorial Association

An engraving of the Great House at Stratford
accompanied an article by John Esten Cooke in the January 24, 1874,
issue of Appleton's Journal. *"You ascend to these observatories*
by flights of stairs leading up from the second floor…
and the view is such as to well reward the visitor
for his trouble," wrote Cooke.

At the beginning of the Civil War,
photographer Mathew Brady retouched a daguerreotype,
which he had taken of Lee in civilian dress about a decade earlier,
to make it appear that Lee was in a military uniform.
This carte de visite *of a youthful-looking Lee is somewhat*
misleading because in the intervening years his hair
had turned gray.

THE MALLEABLE MAN:

ROBERT E. LEE IN THE AMERICAN MIND

EMORY M. THOMAS

Here is a passage from Stephen Vincent Benét's *John Brown's Body*:

> —And so we get the marble man again,
> The head on the Greek coin, the idol-image
> The shape who stands at Washington's left hand,
> Worshipped, uncomprehended and aloof,
> A figure lost to flesh and blood and bones,
> Frozen into legend out of life,
> A blank-verse statue—

This has been the dominant image of Robert E. Lee in the popular mind—Lee as marble, rigid, and remote. Yet the "marble man" has been quite lively, as rendered by those who fashioned and viewed Lee's image in art, as well as by many who wrote about him.

Consider the equestrian statue erected in Richmond in 1890 on what became Monument Avenue. An Ohio-based sculptor initially won the commission, prompting Jubal Early to write Virginia governor Fitzhugh Lee (General Lee's nephew) that if a Yankee executed the work, he would "get together all the surviving members of the Second Corps [of Lee's army] and blow it up with Dynamite." So the sculptor became Jean Antoine Mercié—appropriately from Toulon in deepest southern France, no Yankee from Ohio.

Although hordes of people lauded the statue and the subject, John Mitchell, Jr., an African American member of the Richmond City Council and the editor of the *Richmond Planet*, dissented in print. "The men who talk most about the valor of Lee and the blood of the brave Confederate dead are those who never smelt powder," he wrote. And on the day the statue was unveiled, Mitchell called the event a monument to a "legacy of treason and blood."

Mitchell's was a lonely voice in 1890, but black criticism of Lee's veneration did not end there. In 1999 some people in Richmond built a flood wall beside the James River and planned a tourist attraction. On the wall's twenty-nine panels promoters installed pictures of figures and scenes from Richmond's past. Robert E. Lee's image provoked outrage from Richmond City Council member Sa'ad El Amin, who termed Lee a "Hitler" and a "Stalin" and demanded its removal. Here was an example of the theme: Lee = the Confederacy; the Confederacy = slavery and oppression. The furor inspired much outcry.

During the spring of 2001 a portrait of Lee became a bargaining chip in what some believed was a rightful cause—removing a representation of the battle flag of the Army of Northern Virginia (Lee's army) from the state flag of Georgia.

Practicing traditional Southern virtues—good manners and concern for the feelings of others—Governor Roy Barnes rammed a compromise design for the flag through the General Assembly. Then on Confederate Memorial Day (April 26), the governor unveiled a portrait of Lee restored to the capitol. The portrait was the quid for the pro quo vote of an influential state senator from southern Georgia.

Cast in bronze, carved in marble, or emblazoned on canvas, Robert E. Lee as icon has had a fluid history. He has stood—or, in the case of the Edward Valentine's recumbent statue in the chapel of Washington and Lee, lain—for all manner of causes in the minds of his beholders.

In the written word, as well as in icon, Lee has been both more and less than he was in life. The literary monument surpassing Mercié's and Valentine's statues and everyone's canvases has been Douglas Southall Freeman's four-volume *R. E. Lee: A Biography* (1934–35). Freeman wrote: "Robert Lee was one of the small company of great men in whom there is no inconsistency to be explained, no enigma to be solved. What he seemed, he was—a wholly human gentleman, the essential elements of whose positive character were two and only two, simplicity and spirituality." Freeman concluded his work with the following: "There is no mystery in the coffin there in front of the windows that look to the sunrise."

For a long, long time, Lee (essentially Freeman's "Lee") has been an American hero. And this same Lee has been a secular saint below the Potomac and Ohio rivers. Yet even in the South the Lee paean has never been unanimous. Here, from one region or another, by writers of fiction and nonfiction, are samples of Lee counterpoint.

Allen Tate, writing in 1929 to his friend Andrew Lytle about the frustrations of writing a biography of Lee, said of Lee that he "valued his own honor more than the independence of the South. If he had taken matters in his own hands, he might have saved the situation; he was not willing to do this. It would have violated his Sunday School morality." By 1931 Tate was downright disgusted; he wrote Lytle: "The longer I've contemplated the venerable features of Lee, the more I've hated him. It is as if I had married a beautiful girl, perfect in figure, pure in all those physical attributes that seem to clothe purity of character, and then had found when she had undressed that the hidden places were corrupt and diseased." Not surprisingly, Tate never completed his biography of Lee.

Gertrude Stein wrote in *Everybody's Autobiography* (1937) that Lee was a "weak man." She opined that Lee knew the Confederacy would not win the war and lacked the courage to say what he knew.

Novelist Michael Shaara won a Pulitzer Prize in 1975 for *The Killer Angels* about the battle of Gettysburg. Shaara portrayed Lee as a confused, sad, sick old man who seemed determined to have one more mass bloodletting before he died. The novel became the basis for the 1993 film *Gettysburg*.

I cannot leave the realm of fiction without mentioning what I deem the best work of fiction about Lee, M. A. Harper's *For the Love of Robert E. Lee* (1992). In this book, the teenaged narrator says: "Try to co-opt him now, if you want to. You can't. The line has been broken. Y'all did it. You wouldn't claim him after the war. Fine. He's ours, ours alone, forever and ever, by mutual choice. We chose him and he chose us. We were worth choosing. So the rest of you will just have to make do with Sherman and Grant and the rest of the second-raters. We haven't had any U.S. Presidents until Johnson. We're used to being a joke. The poorest. The baddest. And we are *bad*. Yes, we're bad. But we've got Robert E. Lee, and you can't have him."

In 1960, a quarter-century after Freeman published his opus, historian T. Harry Williams reexamined Lee: "Let us concede that many of the tributes to Lee are deserved. He was not all that his admirers have said of him, but he was a large part of it. But let us also note that even his most fervent admirers, when they come to evaluate him as a strategist, have to admit that his abilities were never demonstrated on a larger scale than a theater."

In subsequent years, other historians analyzed Lee and his image. Thomas L. Connelly published *The Marble Man: Robert E. Lee and His Image in American Society* in 1997. This analysis by a brilliant scholar began in earnest the revisionist critique of Lee as a soldier, saint, and human being. After devoting the bulk of his book to interpreting the Lee image, Connelly offered his version of the Lee reality:

> In truth, Lee was an extremely complex individual. Lee the man has become so intermingled with Lee the hero symbol that the real person has been obscured. Efforts to understand him, and to appraise his capabilities fairly, have been hindered by his image as a folk hero.
>
> Lee was neither serene nor simple. His life was replete with frustration, self-doubt, and a feeling of failure. All these were hidden behind his legendary reserve and his credo of duty and self-control. He was actually a troubled man, convinced that he had failed as a prewar career officer, parent, and moral individual. He suffered the hardships of an unsatisfactory marriage, long absences from his family, and chronic homesickness for his beloved Virginia. He distrusted his own conduct. The specter of family scandals in the past, his unhappy marital situation, his strong Calvinist obsession with sin — all united to make Lee fear for his self-control.

Since Connelly's *Marble Man* and his and Barbara L. Bellows's *God and General Longstreet: The Lost Cause and the Southern Mind* (1982), imitators — pale, in my opinion — have flocked to Connelly's anti-Lee colors. Alan Nolan published *Lee Considered: General Robert E. Lee and Civil War History* in 1991. About this work I confess to have said in print: "Nolan's book reveals a spirit mean and sad, and neither of these adjectives applies to Lee." Then in 2000 came Michael Fellman's *The Making of Robert E. Lee*. Like Connelly and Nolan before him, Fellman seems to me to have been so much in thrall to—and repelled by—the Lee hagiography that he spent most of his energy and ink protesting what Lee was not rather than elucidating who Lee was.

This is but a hasty sample of what artists, writers, historians, and real people have made of Robert E. Lee. Now I believe I have the obligation to state what I believe about the person. The best answer I can offer is my Lee corpus, *Robert E. Lee: A Biography* (1995) and *Robert E. Lee: An Album* (2000). More briefly here, let me offer some thoughts.

I believe that Robert E. Lee was a great man. He was great (1) because of what he did, (2) because of his response to the universal quandary about freedom and control, and (3) because of what I term Lee's comic vision of life.

Lee's deeds were important. Here is Stephen Vincent Benét again:

Yet—look at the face again—look at it well—
This man was not repose, this man was act.
This man who murmured "It is well that war
Should be so terrible, if it were not
We might become too fond of it—" and showed
Himself, for once, completely as he lived
In the laconic balance of that phrase;

This man could reason, but he was a fighter,
Skilful in every weapon of defence
But never retreating while he still could strike,
Dividing a weak force on dangerous ground
And joining it again to beat a strong,
Mocking at chance and all the odds of war
With acts that looked like hairbreadth recklessness
—We do not call them reckless, since they won.
We do not see him reckless for calm
Proportion that controlled the recklessness—
But that attacking quality was there.
He was not mild with life or drugged with justice,
He gripped life like a wrestler with a bull,
Impetuously. It did not come to him
While he stood waiting in a famous cloud,
He went to it and took it by both horns
And threw it down.

Lee was great for the quantity and quality of his accomplishments. Here, in sum, is what he achieved.

He was initially an engineer. He graduated from West Point (1829) second in his class, rechanneled the Mississippi River, opened the upper Mississippi to navigation, won the Mexican War, and captured John Brown and freed Brown's hostages.

Lee was then a warrior. He armed and organized Virginia's troops; found frustration in the Kanawha Valley and on the coasts of South Carolina, Georgia, and Florida; and then came to command; Seven Days, Second Manassas (Bull Run), Sharpsburg (Antietam), Fredericksburg, Chancellorsville, Gettysburg, Bristoe Station, The Wilderness, Spotsylvania, Cold Harbor, Petersburg, Appomattox.

Finally, Lee was an educator. At Washington College (later Washington and Lee University) he introduced elective courses, voluntary chapel, a law school, and a journalism school. And he replaced the myriad rules common to colleges at that time with one rule: "Everyman must be a gentleman."

Here is what Lee did about freedom. He suffered from a huge birth defect—his father, Light Horse Harry Lee—and the negative example of his father drove Lee to restore the family honor and pursue righteousness. I believe that Jean-Jacques Rousseau had it backward when he wrote that people are born free, but are everywhere in chains. Most of us are born in chains—slaves to custom, family, society—to whomever or whatever shapes (warps) our lives. Lee and the rest of us need to get free.

Lee acted out a paradox: to be free, he followed rules and obeyed orders. To his oldest son, Custis, he wrote: "I am fond of independence. It is that feeling that prompts me to come up strictly to the requirements of law & regulations. I wish neither to seek or receive indulgence from any one." Lee controlled himself to liberate himself.

Lee wrote, "The great duty of life is the promotion of the happiness and welfare of our fellow men." Conversely, he believed that sin and wrong were essentially the fruits of selfishness.

Lee was the old man who stared into the face of an infant and intoned, "Teach him to deny himself." It is easy for rigid people to associate Lee with absolutes and overnoble platitudes. But Lee lived beyond conventions and conventional wisdom. Here is what he wrote to Pierre G. T. Beauregard about treason:

> True patriotism sometimes requires of men to act exactly contrary, at one period, to that which it does at another, and the motive which impels them—the desire to do right—is precisely the same. The circumstances which govern their actions change; and their conduct must conform to the new order of things. History is full of illustrations of this. Washington himself is an example. At one time he fought against the French under Braddock, in the service of the King of Great Britain, at another, he fought with the French at Yorktown, under the orders of the Continental Congress of America, against him. He has not been branded by the world with reproach for this; but his course has been applauded.

It may have been no accident that Confederates wore shades of gray.

An appropriate metaphor for Lee's morality is a kite, as portrayed by Wyatt Prunty in his poem "The Kite":

> Vivid for the Sky's emptiness,
> A bright red patch against the haze and blue,
> It soars along a shortened line, but falls

When given run before the wind;

Or like a solitary song's release,
The kite unreels along a spool of thread,
An outward surge over the wind,
Flying by the force of being held.

The single master of a vacant lot,
By pulling down it rises up,
This craft of putting fragile things aloft,
Of letting go and holding on at once.

Lee was act. He acted out his tension between freedom and control. He possessed a comic—as opposed to tragic—vision of life. To his son Custis, who was undergoing a nineteenth-century version of the sophomore slump at West Point, Lee wrote: "Shake off those gloomy feelings. Drive them away, fix your mind & pleasures upon what is before you.... All is bright if you will think it so. All is happy if you will make it so. Do not dream. It is too ideal, too imaginary. Dreaming by day, I mean. Live in the world you inhabit. Look upon things as they are. Take them as you find them. Make the best of them. Turn them to your advantage." And Lee took his own advice. He made the best of every circumstance—personally and professionally.

Lee sought wit and excitement in the company and especially the correspondence of bright, young women. As a young bachelor, Lee had courted a woman named Eliza Mackay. Later, after his own marriage, Lee learned that Eliza was about to marry. On her wedding day, he wrote to her, "But Miss E. how do you feel about this time? Say 12 o'clock of the day, as you see the shadows commence to fall towards the East and know that at last the sun will set?" Interrupted in his writing, Lee returned to his letter four days later. By this time, Eliza was married and Lee asked: "And how did you disport yourself my child? Did you go off well, like a torpedo cracker on Christmas morning?"

Lee attempted to redeem awkward circumstances and bring grace. At St. Paul's Episcopal Church in Richmond in June, 1865, a very large black man first responded to the call to receive communion. Gasp. No one moved, except Lee, who walked forward and knelt beside him.

At one of the worst periods of his life, in December 1863, Lee received at his headquarters a note from Lucy Minnegerode and Lou Haxall, who signed themselves "your two little friends." "We the undersigned," the girls wrote, "write this little note to you our beloved Gen. to ask a little favor of you which if it is in your power to grant we trust you will. We want private Cary Robinson of Com. G. 6th V. Mahone's Brig. to spend his Christmas with us, and if you will grant him a furlough for this purpose we will pay you back in thanks and love and kisses."

The war was going badly. Lee was suffering from what was likely an attack of angina. His wife was crippled, a son captured, a daughter-in-law dying. Moreover, Lee had lost almost all the wealth he ever possessed or controlled. Yet in timely manner, with warmest of hearts, he responded to his "two little friends."

> I rec'd the morning I left camp your joint request for permission to Mr. Cary Robinson to visit you on Xmas, and gave authority for his doing so, provided circumstances permitted. Deeply sympathizing with him in his recent affliction [a death in his family] it gave me great pleasure to extend to him the opportunity of seeing you, but I fear I was influenced by the bribe held out to me, and will punish myself by not going to claim the thanks and love and kisses promised me. I fear too I shall be obliged to submit your letter to Congress, that our Legislators may know the temptations to which poor soldiers are exposed, and in their wisdom devise some means of counteracting its influence. They may know that bribery and corruption is [*sic*] stalking boldly over the land, but may not be aware that the fairest and sweetest are engaged in its practice.

Robert E. Lee was a great man. He forged greatness out of the human condition. That human condition is flawed—as was Lee and are all the rest of us mortals. But Lee did great things. He confronted the universal tension between freedom and control. And despite his legendary reserve and enigmatic posture, he taught us to laugh.

———••••———

Emory M. Thomas is Regents Professor of History Emeritus at the University of Georgia.

*In 1864 Richmond photographer J. W. Davies
took an image of Lee, which became widely circulated in
carte de visite form. This particular likeness, shown here as
an 1875 copy of the original photograph, was the model
for the United States commemorative
stamp issued in 1937.*

IN THE SHADOW OF WASHINGTON:

ROBERT E. LEE AND THE CONFEDERACY

————◆————

RICHARD B. McCASLIN

Robert E. Lee wrote to Pierre G. T. Beauregard in the fall of 1865: "I need not tell you, that true patriotism requires of men sometimes, to act exactly contrary at one period, to that which it does at another." He explained, "[George] Washington himself is an example, at one time he fought against the French, under Braddock, in the service of the King of Great Britain; at another he fought with the French at Yorktown, under the orders of the Continental Congress of America, against him." Reflecting on his own experience, Lee added, "He has not been branded by the world with reproach for this, but his course has been applauded." Condemned by many for his wartime actions, Lee sought reassurance once more in the example set by the leader who served as his role model: "the Great Washington," as Lee's father called the man who was his commander in the American Revolution. Lee consciously lived in the shadow of his hero. Confronted with a chance to lead a revolution, he wore a colonel's uniform like Washington, rode a horse named for one of Washington's favorites, Traveller, packed Washington's sword in his baggage, and tried to win as Washington had done.

Lee, like many Americans of his era, was raised with leaders of the Revolution, especially Washington, as role models. These lessons were reinforced for Lee because his relatives served with Washington. In fact, he thought erroneously that he was born in the same room at Stratford Hall as Richard Henry Lee and Francis Lightfoot Lee, who signed the Declaration of Independence, and he believed correctly that he was christened wearing the same gown their mother had sewn. He spent his early years at Stratford under the steady gaze of portraits of prominent Lees, including revolutionary cousins, and he learned their stories.

Lee could recount the service of many Lees in the Revolution but, more important, he was well-versed in the military career of his father, Henry Lee III. The elder Lee became famous as Light Horse Harry, Washington's favorite cavalry commander. For most of his life, Lee did not know the tragic details of his father's post-Revolution decline, so his reverence endured. He remained receptive to his father's reverence for Washington, which continued even when Light Horse Harry disappeared after being disfigured during the War of 1812. Wandering the West Indies in a futile search for relief, the elder Lee sent letters that stressed the example of his leader, who always supported him and for whom he had delivered an immortal eulogy in Congress.

Light Horse Harry's admonitions were reinforced by his wife, Anne Carter Lee. Left alone to raise her children, Lee's mother emphasized Washington as a role model, just as her father had done. She added a portrait of Washington, presented by him to her grandfather, to the gallery at Stratford, and she treasured the portrait pin that Washington gave her. Anne and her children left Stratford while Robert was young; they settled among Lee's relatives in Alexandria, then a community saturated with Washington's memory. For the town, he had drawn plans, directed the digging of wells, and donated a fire engine. Lee's family attended services at Christ Church, for which Washington had purchased the chandelier. His pew was still there, and the Gospel was read from his Bible. Nearby stood his Masonic lodge and the Carlyle House, where he had joined Edward Braddock for the French and Indian War. Businesses cherished the memory of his patronage, and a museum displayed mementoes.

Lee did not escape the shadow of Washington when he entered West Point in 1825. Washington's headquarters still stood there. Barracks used in the Revolution remained, while the ruins of Fort Putnam, a Revolutionary War outpost, loomed over the school. Lee marched in a review for the Marquis de Lafayette, who also called on Anne. Lee joined a committee that erected a statue of Taddeus Kosciuszko, the Polish-born engineer who served alongside Light Horse Harry and whose cottage stood nearby. Lee even befriended fellow Virginian Joseph E. Johnston, whose father fought under Light Horse Harry. Like his classmates, Lee read about Napoleon, but he also borrowed books on the Revolution from the library.

After graduating with honors from West Point, Lee married Mary Anna Randolph Custis, the daughter of Washington's adopted son, George Washington Parke Custis.

Lee had often visited the Custis home in Arlington, which was filled with Washington memorabilia. Lee enjoyed looking at the treasures and listening to stories related not only by Custis but also by three slaves who had known the commander. At the Lees' marriage, at Arlington, the bride's aunt played a harpsichord given to her by Washington, and guests drank toasts from Washington's punch bowl. As Mary's husband, Lee became a relative of Washington and cultivated close relations with his in-laws as well as with his wife and children. He consoled Custis when Congress rejected his paintings depicting Washington and celebrated with him when Jared Sparks's biography of Washington became a success. To his mother-in-law, Lee confessed that he would be happiest if he too could live among the Washington memorabilia at Arlington, where admittedly his wife and children spent most of their time.

Lee remained in the Army, despite disappointments, and the Mexican War provided a chance to establish himself as the heir of Washington in the Army. He brought Washington's "Revolutionary knives & forks" from Arlington to regale officers at a Christmas banquet, then fought skillfully under Maj. Gen. Winfield Scott. A few years after the war ended, Lee became the superintendent of West Point, where he decorated his office with Washington-related materials from Arlington. Lee and Mary also served dinner at their home with Washington's more refined tableware. Among the guests was Washington Irving, whose work on the former president became one of Lee's favorites to read aloud to Mary, who shared his interest.

Lee chafed as he passed middle age without the opportunity to secure the prestige showered upon Washington. The death of close family members, including his in-laws, did not improve his mood. A stint as a Virginia planter, imposed when the care of Arlington fell to him after his father-in-law died, frustrated Lee as he struggled with debt and unruly slaves. He found some solace in restoring Washington relics, and he aided Mary in the publication of a volume of Washington papers from her father's collection. Lee's service at Harpers Ferry was enhanced for him by his recovery of not only Washington's nephew, who was taken hostage by John Brown, but also one of Washington's swords that Brown's raiders had stolen.

Lee's focus on Washington did not mean that he welcomed secession as an opportunity to lead a revolution. He secluded himself in his room on the Texas frontier in January 1861 to read a new biography of Washington that Mary had sent him, and then wrote to her that Washington's "spirit would be grieved, could he see the wreck of his mighty labors." Lee refused to accept the legality of secession and believed those who urged disunion were actually calling for revolution. This any people had a right to do, but he did not think the circumstances warranted such drastic action. When Texas expelled its federal garrison, Lee returned to Arlington with a heavy heart but nonetheless hosted a dinner in honor of Washington's birthday.

Despite his reservations, when Virginia left the Union in April 1861 and asked Lee to lead, as Washington had, he agreed.

He declined to take charge of forces that might invade the South, especially Virginia, but he accepted the command of Virginia's revolutionaries when the rank was offered to him with the hope "that it will soon be said of you, that you are 'first in peace,' and when that time comes you will have earned the still prouder distinction of being 'first in the hearts of your countrymen.'" Perhaps overwhelmed by this use of his own father's eulogy for Washington, Lee accepted in a speech that one witness recalled as "Washington-like in its modesty." When Virginia then joined the Confederacy, Lee became a Confederate general.

Lee did not immediately become the Washington of the new revolution. Personal losses and defeat dominated the first year of the war for him. Union troops occupied Arlington, taking the Washington relics that the Lees could not send away for safekeeping. Lee himself went to western Virginia, where he failed to defeat the Federals. John A. Washington, the last master of Mount Vernon with the family name, was killed there while serving on Lee's staff. Lee angrily wrote, "Our enemy's have stamped their attack upon our rights with additional infamy by killing the lineal descendant and representative of him who under the guidance of Almighty God established them & by his virtue rendered our Republic immortal." His mood did not improve when he went to South Carolina, where he built fortifications. His return to Richmond as military advisor to Jefferson Davis brought an increase in rank but little else.

Lee's opportunity came with the wounding of Gen. Joseph E. Johnston at Seven Pines on May 31, 1862. Lee took charge of the troops he already referred to as the Army of Northern Virginia. Davis expressed reservations, but Lee convinced him that seizing the initiative by attacking would be an effective way to defend the capital. Maj. Gen. George B. McClellan's position along the Chickahominy River in June 1862 gave Lee a chance to attack and drive away the Federals, but he did not win a decisive victory. His deep disappointment was enhanced by the loss of the White House, the home where George Washington had courted Martha and where Lee's wife briefly found refuge from McClellan's advance. Federals burned the house when they retreated. Lee assumed most of the blame for his military losses, but many Confederates were impressed. In July 1862, the Richmond *Whig* compared Lee to Washington, declaring the former's "modesty is only equalled by his merits."

Lee then overwhelmed Maj. Gen. John Pope, whose blundering provided an irresistible opportunity at Manassas. This triumph allowed Lee to raid northward, where he believed that he could win a decisive victory and force the Federals to negotiate, as Washington had done at Yorktown. Instead, Lee withdrew into Virginia after a bloody standoff at Antietam. He did move quickly to confront McClellan's successor, Maj. Gen. Ambrose E. Burnside, at the Rappahannock River, but a Confederate victory at Fredericksburg in December 1862 provided little solace for a year during which he failed to win his revolution. Lee took scant comfort from the fact that his audacity made him the focus of his cause by 1863, just as Washington had been. Spring brought what many considered to be his finest victory, Chancellorsville, but to him it was yet another hollow triumph because it did not decisively influence the course of the war. Burnside's replacement, Maj. Gen. Joseph Hooker, stalled after enveloping the Army of Northern Virginia, allowing Lee to pummel the separated parts of the Federal army. However, his mood darkened when subordinates allowed Hooker to withdraw safely from the field. Maj. Gen. W. Dorsey Pender bore the brunt of what one of Lee's staff recalled as the "high strong temper of a Washington."

Hooker's defeat allowed Lee to launch another raid into the North to seek a decisive victory. He believed that this would make events elsewhere, such as Vicksburg, matter little. As he told others, he intended to fight a battle that, if won, would secure independence. When his divisions met Union cavalry and infantry at Gettysburg, he hurried to the battlefield with this in mind. Lt. Gen. James Longstreet, commander of Lee's I Corps, reminded his leader of the heavy losses at Chancellorsville and urged him to slip south into a defensive position. Determined to win a decisive victory, and aware that this could not be achieved by staying on the defensive, Lee ordered several unsuccessful attacks that climaxed with the repulse of Pickett's Charge.

Criticism of Lee emerged after Gettysburg, but he insisted that he could still win. To encourage his troops during the cold winter of early 1864, he issued a declaration that read in part: "SOLDIERS! You tread with no unequal step the road by which your fathers marched through suffering, privation and blood to independence. Continue to emulate in the future, as you have in the past, their valour in arms, their patient endurance of hardships, their high resolve to be free, which no trial could shake, no bribe seduce, no danger appall, and be assured that the just God who crowned their efforts with success will, in His own good time, send down His blessing upon yours." His men noticed the historical references; as Col. Clement A. Evans wrote in his diary, "Lee is regarded by his army as nearest approaching the character of the great & good Washington than any man living."

Lee realized by the spring of 1864 that he probably could not win a decisive victory, but that did not preclude prolonging the war until the North sued for peace. After bloody engagements in which Lee inflicted heinous but easily replaced casualties on Gen. Ulysses S. Grant's army, Lee was forced into the trenches at Richmond. He may well have realized the supreme irony that his depleted army, as Emory M. Thomas later wrote, "had attempted to duplicate the strategy of Washington, only to find themselves at the last in the position of Lord Cornwallis." It was with reluctance that, in February 1865, Lee accepted the rank held by Washington during the Revolution: general-in-chief. His second general order asked his troops to keep fighting "with the firm assurance that He who gave freedom to our fathers will bless the efforts of their children to preserve it." A few days later, he again assured his soldiers that "with the liberty transmitted by their forefathers they have inherited the spirit to defend it." His words brought declarations of support from many of his regiments as well as from Richmond newspapers, all of which once again compared him favorably to Washington.

By 1865 sustaining the war in the trenches was not possible, so Lee met with Davis. According to the latter, Lee informed him, "In language similar to that employed by Washington during the Revolution," that if he were allowed to retreat to the mountains of western Virginia, he could last twenty years. A concept first proposed by Lee in 1862, it was a feeble echo of a proposal by Washington had once made. But Washington never resorted to such a desperate measure, and Lee, when he moved west, was surrounded and forced to surrender.

Lee's failure as a revolutionary leader crushed him, but he never abandoned Washington as a role model. Shortly before Lee wrote to Beauregard in late 1865, he accepted the presidency of Washington College, which he and others mistakenly believed had been founded by the revolutionary commander himself. Lee never entered politics, despite numerous requests, but he played the role of statesman, working for the preservation of Washington's Union while also laboring to recover Washington relics lost from Arlington. He never wrote his own story, but he edited a second edition of Light Horse Harry's memoirs and helped Mary publish an expanded version of the slim volume of Washington papers from her father's collection. After Lee's death in 1870, many likened him to Washington in an effort to justify the Confederacy. Scholars have suggested that these comparisons were in fact invented long after the war by those who sought to justify the Lost Cause. In fact, Lee might not have welcomed comparisons that led Virginia to place his statue alongside that of Washington in the national Capitol, but during his life he did much to forge an enduring link with the role model in whose shadow he remains.

<hr />

Richard B. McCaslin is Associate Professor of History at the University of North Texas.

Michael Strieby Nachtrieb, an Ohio-born artist,
fought for the Union in the Civil War for three years.
After the war, he opened a studio in New York where
he painted portraits of famous politicians, actors, bishops,
and educators. Lee's daughter Mary Custis claimed
"It is the best portrait of my father."

ROBERT E. LEE
AND JEFFERSON DAVIS

WILLIAM C. DAVIS

Jefferson Davis and Robert E. Lee first met in 1825 at the U.S. Military Academy at West Point. Davis stood a year ahead of Lee, yet it was Lee who would come to stand as the ideal of all cadets. Davis, one given at that time of his youth to hero worship, probably looked up to the younger Lee, but only from afar. Lee, after all, came from the bluest of bloods, with a name known in almost every literate household in America. Moreover, Lee would be the exemplary cadet, graduating second in his class of 1829. Davis, on the other hand, was almost the typical fraternity boy, court martialled and dismissed once for being caught at an off-limits tavern, reinstated, and then nearly killed when he fell down a steep slope while sneaking back to the post drunk after a visit to the same tavern, and finally narrowly averting irrevocable dismissal and disgrace during the famous "egg nog" riot of 1826.

When Davis—almost miraculously—graduated in 1828 in the bottom third of his class, he would not see Lee for at least two decades. When war came with Mexico, Davis joined Zachary Taylor's army at Saltillo in January 1847 as colonel of the First Mississippi Rifles. Lee was there at the same time, but if they saw each other, neither ever mentioned it. Nevertheless, Davis did not remain unaware of Lee during the war or the years that followed. Both emerged from the Mexican War as heroes, though Davis's notoriety outstripped Lee's. In 1855, when now-Secretary of War Davis created the Second U.S. Cavalry, he gave Lee its choice lieutenant colonelcy, just one grade behind its commander, Davis's life-long hero and idol, Albert Sidney Johnston.

Davis continued to pay careful attention to Lee when the Civil War broke out. From the new Confederate capital in Montgomery, Alabama, he tried to build his infant army. Five days after the secession of Virginia, Davis wired Governor John Letcher to ask Lee's whereabouts, though he had been kept informed of Lee's activities for some days beforehand. There was never a question in Davis's mind that he wanted Lee with him. When Davis and the government moved to Richmond in late May 1861, Lee was one of those he first sought out. Indeed, well before then he had tried to get Lee to come to Montgomery to confer with him, but the growing emergency on Virginia's Potomac front kept Lee in place. Even so, Lee's very first wartime communication to Davis exposed part of the bedrock of their future relationship. Along with other questions in a prior communication from the president, Davis had asked Lee if he felt any unease about the fact that his commission as a major general was in the Virginia state forces, whereas once Virginia was in the Confederacy, he would be superseded by brigadiers commissioned by the regular national army, such as Joseph E. Johnston. If the question had been asked of Johnston, he would have turned apoplectic. Lee simply replied that "my commission in Virginia [is] satisfactory to me." When Davis was already starting to have problems with ambitious men seemingly more interested in rank and reputation than in serving their new nation, such modesty and subordination made Lee a man of mark before he had yet heard a gun fired.

Familiarity during the first year of the war bridged whatever gap may have existed between Davis and Lee. Davis did not love Lee as he had the now-dead Sidney Johnston, but he respected Lee's ability and believed that he could rely upon and work with him. For his part, Lee judged his commander-in-chief brilliantly. He knew of Davis's feuds with other officers during the Pierce administration. He observed firsthand the breakdown in relations between the president and both Joseph E. Johnston and Pierre J. T. Beauregard, as well as others. In none of these disagreements did Davis hold exclusive title to blame, but he owned a good share of it in all of them, and for a man with Lee's keen insight into character, lessons were drawn. A man could get along with Jefferson Davis if he observed a few simple rules: Do not question him unless he invited criticism. Do not challenge him. Keep him fully informed at all times. Do not assail his friends or cronies. Have nothing to do with the press, and eschew all public controversy. Avoid politicians, especially those in the growing anti-Davis camp. Most of all, remain loyal. These were requirements of anyone who expected to get along with him, but especially of subordinates. No man on earth who enjoyed Davis's friendship would ever have a more loyal friend, but Davis expected that loyalty to be returned in kind. Happily, in almost every respect, these requirements accorded with Lee's own notions of the proper deportment of a general to his commander-in-chief.

As a result, Robert E. Lee was ideally suited to be Davis's commanding general in the days before Johnston was wounded, and now Lee was better equipped than any other man in the Confederacy to manage both the army and the president. In short, though he may not have realized it, Lee was a better politician and statesman than Davis. He knew how to subordinate his own pride to the greater goal of getting what he needed from men, whether his lieutenants or his superiors. He would even show that he knew how to be a sycophant at times, giving Davis more flattery than did most other generals of the war, and on Davis's most prideful topic, his military judgment.

The way in which Lee nurtured his relationship with Davis is worth considering in some detail. Better than anyone else, Lee knew that Joseph Johnston's greatest failing was his refusal to communicate with Davis. Johnston's feeble excuse was the fear that if he suggested anything to Davis, he would then be committed to carrying it out whether he wished to or not. Moreover, when it came to fighting or responsibility, Johnston, like Bartleby the scrivener, generally "preferred not to." On June 5, just four days after assuming command of what he would soon style the Army of Northern Virginia,

Lee wrote Davis a very full letter outlining all of his thoughts and closing with the comforting expression that "our position requires you should know everything." Better yet, Lee then *apologized* for troubling Davis with more information than he might want, a brilliant touch. A few days later, as he struggled to reinforce Thomas J. Jackson in the Shenandoah Valley, Lee "proposed" such a movement to Davis, yet asked the president to decide. Henceforward, expressions such as "I need not tell you," or "do you think anything can be done," or "what do you think of the propriety of," and most humble and flattering of all, "I shall feel obliged to you for any directions you may think proper to give," appeared in many of Lee's letters. These and similar expressions may have been nothing more than sincerely felt questions, but it cannot be denied that by their wording and use they also, whether by chance or premeditation, consistently reinforced Lee's attitude of respect and subordination to the president. At the same time they salved Davis's ego and helped, in part, to ease the president's frustration over not being at the front, where of all places he would have preferred to be.

Another facet of Lee's character, and of his perfect alignment with Davis's personality, became evident as the war progressed. When Lee failed to achieve complete success in any of his campaigns, as he failed to bag McClellan completely at the end of the Peninsula fighting, he took the responsibility squarely onto his own shoulders. "I fear all was not done that might have been done to harass and destroy our enemies," he told Davis, "but I blame nobody but myself." Now following upon the crushing defeat at Gettysburg, Lee took all of the responsibility upon himself and asked to be allowed to resign. Nothing was better calculated to win Davis's undying regard. Lee's letter touched him deeply. It reminded him of his dead hero Sidney Johnston, and how he had always said that "success is the test of merit," and how he had borne in silence the clamor of uncomprehending critics such as those now blaming Lee for the defeat. "My dear friend," Davis responded, "there is nothing which I have found to require a greater effort of patience than to bear the criticisms of the ignorant." From his greater experience at being the object of calumny, he advised Lee to ignore it. As for resignation and replacement, Lee had no equal, he told him, much less a superior. "To ask me to substitute you by someone in my judgment more fit to command," said Davis, "is to demand an impossibility."

Instead of having his confidence in Lee diminished by defeat, Davis only felt it increase. More and more now he thought of Lee when he looked to other theaters of the war where his confidence was sorely tested, if not eradicated. The Army of Tennessee was a trouble spot almost from the beginning of the conflict, thanks chiefly to Braxton Bragg's peculiar unfitness for command. With that army practically in rebellion against its commander by August 1863, and with a campaign against Rosecrans under way, Davis thought of sending Lee west to assume the command. Lee declined on several grounds, and the president accepted. But then later in August he called Lee to Richmond to discuss the matter again, and again Lee declined. Davis was a man who knew what he wanted, but this general held a special place in his affections and had his respect, and he resisted exercising his raw authority to compel his best commander to do something against his wishes. Davis did, however, finally send James Longstreet and most of the First Corps to Tennessee, even though Lee asked that it not be done, and when the president once again expressed a desire that Lee go along with Longstreet, he took Lee's refusal as final. As Lee remained in Virginia, sparring with Meade in the months of relative inactivity following Gettysburg, Davis visited the army frequently to confer with the general. While there, they were often seen going to church together. The professional relationship was blossoming into a warm friendship, at least on Davis's part. Interestingly, one searches almost in vain in Lee's wartime correspondence to find evidence of his personal feelings toward, or opinion of, the president.

By the end of 1864, when even Lee had not been able to hold back the legions of the Union and as Richmond lay besieged, Davis's popularity within the Confederate hierarchy fell to an all-time low. There were calls for his removal, by impeachment if possible, by extralegal means if necessary. Rumors surfaced suggesting that Lee should take office in Davis's place, even become dictator, in the emergency. Lee refused to countenance such nonsense, nor even to give evidence that he knew of such thoughts. He remained loyal to Davis in the dark days just as Davis had always been loyal to him, though now, for the first and only time in the war, their relationship appears to have suffered a severe strain. It started with that perennial running sore, Joseph Johnston. Davis had removed him after it became evident that he would not try to hold Atlanta. His replacement, John Bell Hood, failed as well, and then almost lost his army in Tennessee. When he had to be replaced, once more, like a recurring nightmare, there was only Johnston. General-in-chief again by February 1865, Lee tried his best to make it easier for Davis to swallow Johnston. On his own authority, he asked to have Johnston assigned to the command, but pointedly added that Johnston would be reporting directly to him. Davis saw some hope in this. It relieved him from the odium of acting on his own to reinstate Johnston—he was simply granting his general-in-chief's request on a matter quite within that general's area of responsibility. He also continued to hope that where he and Johnston had failed to be able to work together, perhaps Johnston and Lee would be able, a vain hope as it proved.

Still it cost Davis much inwardly to see his old nemesis given the honor of another army command, and this left him testy a few days later when he asked Lee to come into Richmond to confer with him on a matter of secondary import. Probably frustrated at Davis's frequent calls for hand-holding conferences and increasing unwillingness to address the realities of the Confederacy's dreadful situation, Lee failed for once to respond as he always had in the past. If sources can be believed, the general replied that he could not spare the time. The response hurt and angered Davis, who shot back a reply that the general might "rest assured I will not ask your views in answer to measures. Your counsels are no longer wanted in this matter." It smacks of nothing so much as the response of a hurt child. Lee immediately sensed that he had hurt the president's feelings. He went to see him after all, and though their correspondence temporarily took on a cooler tone—Davis ceased addressing him as "my dear friend" for a while—the injury was soon forgotten. Davis just needed to talk to Lee for security and support. He needed to have his friend with him for comfort in those darkening hours.

Lee realized long before Davis that the cause was lost. Indeed, as 1865 wore on he almost marveled at the president's continuing optimism that somehow a victory would be wrested from the Yankees and freedom achieved. "The President is very pertinacious in opinion and purpose," Lee told an associate then, showing a "remarkable faith in the possibility of still winning our independence." He might better have called it obstinacy, if not a retreat from reality. Yet when Davis seized a new potential weapon for winning that independence—the idea of enlisting blacks to fight in Confederate armies—Lee enthusiastically supported him. Indeed, three years later Lee would claim that he told Davis often and repeatedly as early as 1862 that the slaves should be emancipated. He believed it would strengthen Confederate hopes abroad and weaken the moral arguments advanced by the Union, but Davis "would not hear of it." Perhaps so. Certainly Lee embraced the idea of raising Negro regiments, but for all of them it was too little too late.

Finally came the fateful loss of Five Forks and the evacuation of Richmond. Davis and Lee spent some of that last day together, as they had met occasionally during the last of March, often at the home of the Rev. Charles Minnegerode. The minister could not but note at the dinner table, "It was sad to see these two men with their terrible responsibilities upon them and the hopeless outlook." When Lee arrived during one dinner, all the other diners left the room and closed the door behind them, leaving Lee and the president "to consult in lonely conference." That April was the last time Lee and Davis saw one another for the next year and one-half.

We all know what followed for the two of them. For Davis, an attempt to reach the western Confederacy, his capture, and two years of imprisonment leading to a trial that was never completed, and finally his release, to wander England and Europe, and then the South for years before finally he settled in Mississippi once more. For Lee, a quiet surrender at Appomattox, a return first to his Richmond home, and then a measure of peace in Lexington before his early death in 1870, worn out by the war and its strains on a weakened heart. Never during those years or afterward did Davis utter a single reproachful word about Lee for Appomattox, nor for any other episode of his career. Rather, Davis became an enthusiastic contributor to the Lee legend, and one of his most ardent defenders. Lee, on the other hand, as he had during the war, largely kept his views of the president to himself. He did speak critically, and in confidence, only twice that we know of. In 1869 he told a painter that, while he admired Davis's sterling qualities of character, he believed that the president was, "of course, one of the extremist politicians." A year earlier, speaking to a confidant, Lee observed that despite his high regard for Davis, he still blamed him for being so confrontational with opponents like Johnston and Beauregard and thereby failing to unite everyone to the single purpose of the cause. "Mr. Davis' enemies became so many," said Lee, "as to destroy his power and to paralyze the country."

Nothing was said of this at their first meeting after the war—and what would prove to be their last. Lee was called to testify in Davis's trial, in the hope that his testimony would help to place the full responsibility for all Confederate activities on its former president. Lee refused to play the game. "I am responsible for what I did," he said on the witness stand, "and I cannot now recall any important movement I made which I would not have made had I acted entirely on my own responsibility." That ended any usefulness Lee might have had for the prosecution. This straightforward, manly acceptance of his own responsibility was to be the last thing Davis ever heard from his beloved general's lips.

In 1863 Davis had written to his brother Joseph that "a General in the full acceptation of the word is a rare product, scarcely more than one can be expected in a generation, but in this mighty war in which we are engaged there is need for half a dozen." In the end, Davis really got only one, Robert E. Lee. And for whatever he may be blamed for shortening the war in the decisive Western Theater by his adherence first to Bragg and then his deadly dance of command with Joseph E.

Johnston, it is inarguable that in the Eastern Theater, Davis prolonged the war if by no other single fact than his unwavering and unyielding support for Lee. It is often forgotten that Lee came to command with an unenviable war record behind him. Many thought him too timid, others believed him not entirely committed to the cause, and in Virginia and South Carolina especially he had been dubbed derisively "Granny" and "Spades" Lee. Davis was not obliged to give him command of the Army of Northern Virginia, and might not have but for his disillusionment with G. W. Smith, and Smith's own psychosomatic ailments whenever under pressure. But once Lee was in command, Davis quickly realized his worth and stood by him, even when he confided to Varina that on the Peninsula, Lee had not achieved all that the president had hoped for. Through the near loss of most of his army at Antietam and the crushing defeat at Gettysburg, the president never once wavered in his attachment to Lee. Furthermore, by resisting the clamor to send Lee to the troubled Army of Tennessee—and his own desire to do so—Davis kept in place the one man who knew his army and countryside better than any other. Moreover, Davis listened to Lee, in time taking his counsel almost as if it had come from lips of Sidney Johnston himself, whom he always believed might have been an even greater general had he lived. Davis did not interfere with Lee's army, gave him the generals he wanted for his corps and divisions, and bent every effort to send him the regiments he needed.

For his part, Lee read his commander-in-chief brilliantly, and showed a maturity and a devotion to cause above self that would have shamed most other high-ranking commanders. While Johnston would whimper over his rank and spend most of the war complaining, and while Beauregard preened and blustered and took every opportunity to politick behind the back of a president who had the audacity to think he outranked the great Beauregard, Lee consistently subordinated himself to his goals. He realized that his mission was not to pamper his own ego or advance his reputation. He had a job to get done with his army, and the best way to achieve it was to have the full support and confidence of his commander-in-chief. If that meant flattering the president, he would do it. If that meant allowing Davis to think that Lee's ideas were sometimes his own, so be it. If it meant taking precious time while on an arduous campaign to write the president a letter when there was nothing to say, Lee would do it. If it meant simply being a friend and helping a man deal with a crushing burden even greater than Lee's, then the general knew what he had to do. Sycophantic at times? Yes. Fawning, even, now and then? Yes. Counterproductive or wasteful of time? Never. Lee's eye was on his mission, and he knew better than anyone else how much stronger was his steel if he had the president behind his weapons rather than in front of them.

And thus, these two very different men, who in another time or under different circumstances probably would not— could not—have been friends, achieved a synergy that helped to keep the Confederacy afloat in the East far longer than could have been expected with any of the other full-rank generals of the South in command. In the understanding and rapport they achieved and in the way they cooperated, Davis and Lee formed a model civil-military team surpassing any other of the war, even Lincoln and Grant, and matched in our national history only by that between Franklin D. Roosevelt and George C. Marshall in World War II.

———•••►———

William C. Davis is Professor of History and Director of Programs at the Virginia Polytechnic Institute and State University.

*Photographer Michael Miley took this full-length
portrait of Lee around 1869, when he was president
of Washington College. At this time, Lee was suffering the effects
of chronic heart disease and, not long after, he told sculptor
Edward V. Valentine, "I feel that I have an incurable disease
coming on me—old age. I would like to go to some
quiet place in the country and rest."*

ROBERT E. LEE:
NATIONAL SYMBOL

◄••••►

JAMES I. ROBERTSON, JR.

On Wednesday, April 12—as his army officially laid down its arms, Robert E. Lee departed Appomattox for Richmond. He found the capital a scene of widespread destruction. Confederate officials had begun abandoning Richmond on the night of April 2–3, when the flames of military supplies set afire raged out of control and swept through the city. The entire downtown area was destroyed. Symbolically, Richmond went up in smoke with the Confederacy.

Lee headed toward the Franklin Street home where his family had resided for most of the war. It had barely survived flames that had swept to within a block. As Lee rode across the pontoon bridge into Richmond early in the morning, large crowds of silent Virginians, Union soldiers, and dislocated African Americans gathered along the route. "There was no excitement, no hurrahing," one eyewitness noted, "but as the great chief passed, a deep, loving murmur, greater than these, rose from the very heart of the crowd. Taking off his hat, and simply bowing his head, the man great in adversity passed silently to his own door; it closed

55

upon him; and his people had seen him for the last time in his battle harness."

Lee had no job or income. His beloved Virginia had been destroyed. Desolation and poverty were upon the land. Lee was exhausted in mind and body. Perhaps he felt that the sorrows of the whole South were his burden. From the day of surrender, Lee had decided to remain in Virginia. The state offered little for the future. Yet, Virginia was home. He told a friend: "Now, more than any other time, Virginia and every state in the South needs us. We must try and, with as little delay as possible, go to work and build up their prosperity." Lee also declined an invitation to visit Europe for an extended stay. "I cannot desert my native state in the hour of her adversity," he stated. "I must abide her fortunes, and share her fate."

There was no bitterness in defeat. Lee was above that. "All should unite," he declared, "in honest efforts to obliterate the effects of war, and to restore the blessings of peace." He determined to set the example himself.

Lee regularly attended services at St. Paul's Episcopal Church in Richmond. Some African Americans attended services, but the seating was segregated. On Sunday the minister invited the faithful to come forth and receive communion at the chancel railing. A well-dressed black man walked forward. The congregation seemed to freeze. The man knelt alone at the railing—until Lee walked calmly from his pew and knelt beside him. The congregation quickly followed suit.

By summer Lee was anxious to leave Richmond. The city was too full of people, noise, and confusion. He wanted to buy some land in the country, move there, and try to live the quiet life of a retired farmer. Mrs. Elizabeth Randolph Cocke, a wealthy widow, invited the Lees to occupy a small house on her James River estate above Richmond. The home, named Derwent, was not elaborate, but it was adequate. For two months Lee and his family enjoyed the solitude.

Meanwhile, the trustees at Washington College in Lexington were seeking a president. They had precious little to offer. The school had been a small, respectable institution at the southern end of the Shenandoah Valley. In 1864 Federal soldiers had ransacked the campus, scattered the contents of the library, destroyed laboratory equipment, and left the buildings heavily damaged. Its previous students had mostly joined the army. Only forty-five male students and four faculty members remained.

The trustees needed a prominent person at the head for fundraising. So poor was the place that Judge John W. Brockenbrough, rector of the board of trustees, had to borrow a suit of clothes and fifty dollars to ride to Derwent and offer the presidency to Lee.

Lee hesitated. The position offered neither fortune nor fame. His previous academic experience as superintendent at West Point had not been pleasant. Lee also knew that many in the North regarded him as a traitor and the most dangerous of all the ex-Confederates. Such feelings would not help the school.

The encouragement of friends was a factor in Lee's decision. So were the sentiments he later explained in a letter to his wife: "Life is indeed gliding away and I have nothing of good to show for mine that is past. I pray I may be spared to accomplish something for the benefit of mankind and to the honour of God."

Lee accepted the offer to become a college president. He informed the trustees, "I think it is the duty of every citizen, in the present condition of the Country, to do all in his power to aid in the restoration of peace and harmony.... It is particularly incumbent on those charged with the instruction of the young to set them an example of submission to authority." Lee stated his personal feelings in simple terms. "I have a self-imposed task which I must accomplish. I have led the young men of the South in battle; I have seen many of them die on the field; I shall devote my remaining energies to training young men to do their duty in life."

In mid-September Lee arrived in Lexington and assumed his new post. He recalled West Point and how everything there was organized and everyone was part of a distinct chain of command. Now, at Washington College, Lee held a blank sheet of paper and looked at confusion and uncertainty. Yet he instantly showed that he would be a hands-on president, not a figurehead. One of his first tasks was to review the qualities of each faculty member and to interview each student personally.

Contributions flowed into the school from admirers of Lee. Former abolitionist Henry Ward Beecher raised funds. Cyrus McCormick, inventor of the first grain reaper only a few miles from Lexington, was a leading contributor. By the end of Lee's first year in office, the school had received over $100,000. The faculty increased from four to fourteen, while enrollment doubled to more than one hundred students. Lee established ten areas of study, liberalized the overall curriculum, laid the groundwork for a law school, and watched with pleasure the construction of a campus chapel.

The president also introduced an "honor code" of behavior whereby he "treated the students as gentlemen and expected them to act as gentlemen." Lee's discipline of "my boys" (as he called the students) consisted of a fatherly talk rather than a customary paddling. One student, called before Lee for misconduct, later confessed, "I wish he had whipped me. I could have stood it better. But he talked to me so kindly, and so tenderly, about my mother, and the sacrifices which she, a widow, is making to send me to college, and of how I ought to appreciate her love… that the first thing I knew I was blubbering like a baby."

Few college presidents ever worked harder for the religious good of students. To one local minister, Lee remarked: "I shall fail in the leading object that brought me here, unless these young men become real Christians." He repeated similar thoughts to another clergyman: "I dread the thought of any student going away from the College without becoming a sincere Christian."

At the same time, Lee silenced many of his northern enemies by twice testifying before congressional committees in Washington. At one point, he accepted an invitation for a brief meeting with Grant, now president, in the White House. Lee was always ready to give counsel on the future to former Confederates. The advice never varied: Forget the passions of the past, and live in peace as loyal Americans.

When Lee applied for a pardon, he was unaware that an oath of allegiance had to be taken by all former Confederate officers. Shortly after the war, Lee signed an oath and mailed it to Washington. The government, for unknown reasons, never acknowledged receipt. The mistake was not discovered until 1975, when Congress granted Lee a pardon.

The Washington College years were not especially happy ones for the general. "Traveller is my only companion," Lee observed. "I may also say my pleasure. He and I, whenever practicable, wander out in the mountains and enjoy sweet confidence." Occasionally, those short trips took him to the Lexington cemetery. There Lee would stand in thought beside the grave of his great lieutenant Thomas "Stonewall" Jackson.

The college president's health was slowly failing, his wife's arthritic condition was totally crippling, and the struggle to resurrect the college from the ashes of war was both long and tedious. While he was not happy, Lee did feel fulfilled. He was doing his duty, which now was to educate the young rather than lead them into battle.

Lee's confidence rested on history. He wrote Col. Charles Marshall, his wartime aide: "The truth is this: The march of Providence is so slow and our desires so impatient; the work of progress is so immense and our means of aiding it so feeble; the life of humanity is so long, [and] that of the individual so brief, that we often see only the ebb of the advancing wave and are thus discouraged. It is history that teaches each of us to hope."

Lee continually impressed everyone who met him. He refused to use liquor, tobacco, or profanity. Perhaps because he was such a doting father, none of his three surviving daughters ever married. Esteemed as a model Southerner, Lee was always in demand at functions. Yet he shunned large gatherings and public acclaim.

In 1867 the radical Republican-controlled Congress placed the South under military occupation. "Reconstruction" thus began. Lee again took the lead in advising peace and dignity rather than anger and revenge. A Confederate widow voiced deep hatred for all Yankees. The commander who had led armies against the North replied calmly: "Madam, do not train your children in hostility to the government of the United States. Remember, we are all one country now. Dismiss from your mind all sectional feeling, and bring them up to be Americans."

Possibly the most startling event of Lee's postwar years came in 1868, when the *New York Herald* endorsed him for president of the United States. The newspaper did so on the grounds that Lee was a better man in every way than Republican candidate Ulysses S. Grant. Lee ignored the matter, as he did all politics.

Washington College grew steadily in both size and prestige. The campus now boasted twenty professors and four hundred students. Yet the strain of war proved too great even for Lee's strong heart. Soon after the 1869–70 school year began, the general's heart ailment became more pronounced. He was in bed for several days. Once back at his duties, he began to experience difficulty breathing. Lee's condition grew so serious that the faculty begged him to take a vacation.

The trip that Lee undertook in spring 1870 through the Deep South was done presumably to improve his health, but it was more likely a farewell tour. Lee sensed that he was dying. He visited familiar settings and old friends. He even agreed to sit for a portrait and pose for a statue.

When school began in September, Lee was only sixty-three years old. But he looked older, with his snow-white hair, a slight stoop, slow walk, and apparently constant fatigue. The general was saying grace at dinner on September 28 when he suffered a paralyzing stroke. At 9:30 A.M. on October 12, the painful breathing ceased. Robert E. Lee's earthly campaigns were over.

Lee's death prompted national mourning. A New York City newspaper, with every reason to damn Lee forever, stated at his passing: "In him the military genius of America was developed in a greater extent than ever before. In him all that was pure and lofty in mind and purpose found lodgment. He came nearer the ideal of a soldier and Christian general than any man we can think of."

Hundreds of eulogies appeared in every corner of the land. None was more moving, or more simple, than that from Julia Ward Howe. The northern woman who had sent Union soldiers confidently into battle with the words of "The Battle Hymn of the Republic" wrote of Lee:

A gallant foeman in the fight,
A brother when the fight was o'er,
The hand that led the host with might
The blessed torch of learning bore…
Thought may the minds of men divide,
Love makes the heart of nations one,
And so, thy soldier grave beside,
We honor thee, Virginia's son.

Lee was buried in the college chapel. Trustees quickly changed the name of the school from Washington College to Washington and Lee University. To this day, however, many of its graduates refer to it as "General Lee's College."

Five years as a college president may well stand as the crowning achievement of Lee's life. A terrible civil war had fractured the United States, and the wounds seemed too deep for any healing. Half of the nation stood in the humiliation of defeat. Then Lee stepped forward. The general, one writer summarized, "was the only man who had the chance to do it all—save the South's pride, give the South the calm example that would guide it in a stormy postwar period, and do it all in a way that the North would first approve and then applaud."

Lee was forced to make imperfect choices in an imperfect world. Great in war, greater after war, Lee asked no pardon for doing any wrong. He was a man seemingly always at peace with himself, whether it was in leading soldiers into legend or carrying a nation into the dawn of a new day.

———•••———

James I. Robertson, Jr. is Alumni Distinguished Professor of History at Virginia Polytechnic Institute and State University.

Artist Thomas Nast of Morristown, New Jersey,
completed this pen-and-ink drawing, "Peace in Our Country,"
in 1890 to commemorate the unveiling of the Lee Monument
in Richmond, Virginia. During the Civil War, Nast was
so famous for his political cartoons supporting the Union
that President Abraham Lincoln called him
"our best recruiting sergeant."

IN HONOR
OF ROBERT E. LEE

—————

CHARLES P. ROLAND

*Delivered October 12, 1996, at Washington and Lee University
in the Lee Chapel on the anniversary of Robert E. Lee's death.*

We are gathered here today to observe the anniversary of the
death of Robert E. Lee. We are here also to honor his memory,
for we believe he was both a great general and a great man.
We come in full cognizance of the fierce conflict that raged in
Lee's soul when he was forced to decide whether to fight
against or for his state and people. Answering the call of
sentiments grounded in a profound sense of kinship and
loyalty to neighborhood, and following his own pervasive
sense of honor and duty, Lee made the fateful choice of fighting for Virginia and the Confederacy. "I cannot raise my hand
against my birthplace, my home, my children," he said. "Save
in defence of my native state, I never again desire to draw
my sword." He could well have repeated the words of his
father, Gen. Light Horse Harry Lee, when faced with a similar
decision, declared, "Virginia is my country. Her will I obey,
however lamentable the fate to which it may subject me."

Robert E. Lee's decision ultimately cost the nation thousands of northern and southern lives. Eminent scholars of American history have speculated that Lee might have ended the Civil War in one year had he chosen to fight for the North, which he had the option of doing. For his decision, Lee also had to pay a terrible price. Probably, he would have been victorious as the leader of the Union forces, and fame and honors would have been his reward; possibly—one is tempted to say probably—he would have been elevated to the presidency of the United States.

Instead, many have subjected Lee to the epithet of "traitor." Only a few days ago, regrettably, I read in a book review published in the *New York Times* a statement calling him a "bloodstained traitor." The meaning of the word "traitor," of course, depends upon one's point of view. To an established nation any separatist movement not approved by the national government itself is, by definition, traitorous. By such a definition, Lee's father was a bloodstained traitor to the British government, as were George Washington and all the other Americans who fought against the mother country during the American war for independence. Today they are hailed as our great founding patriots.

In one of the most striking ironies of American history, Abraham Lincoln, the nemesis of the seceded South, uttered an eloquent and sweeping justification of revolution and secession. The time was 1847, not 1860 or 1861. He did not use the word secession; and obviously, he was not speaking of the withdrawal of a state or states from the United States.

Lincoln's declaration endorsing secession occurred in a discussion of affairs leading to the Mexican War, but the statement was universal in its scope and principles. He said, "Any people anywhere, being inclined and having the power, have the right to rise up, and shake off the existing government, and form a new one that suits them better. This is a most valuable — a most sacred right — a right, which we hope and believe, is to liberate the world. Nor is this right confined to cases in which the whole people of an existing government may choose to exercise it. Any portion of such people that can, may revolutionize, and make their own, of so much of the territory as they inhabit." Of course, the operative words here are "having the power." As events turned out, the cause for which Lee fought did not command sufficient power to sustain itself against the might of the Union, but certainly, the conditions for separation set forth by Lincoln entitled any people, including Lee and his fellow Confederates, to the right to attempt it.

My point in mentioning these matters is to illustrate that simplistic and invidious names and definitions will not suffice in a discourse on such momentous affairs as movements for independence. Upright and conscientious men disagreed to the ultimate extent on the issues leading to the Civil War; finally, these issues could be resolved only by the ordeal of battle. In that tremendous conflict, friend often opposed friend, brother opposed brother, and child opposed parent. Lee made his choice (the choice of Hercules, the writer Thomas Nelson Page called it) and stood ready to accept the results when the war ended in his defeat.

In defeat, Lee the great general became Lee the great man; or perhaps I should say the greater man, for unquestionably his greatness as a general grew out of his strength of character as a man. The visible transition from great general to great man began in the event of his surrender. Refusing to dismiss his troops with their arms and encourage them to resort to guerrilla warfare, he said, "The question is, is it right to surrender this army? If it is right, then I will take the responsibility." And finally, "We must consider the effect [of guerrilla warfare] on the country as a whole... we would bring on a state of affairs it would take the country years to recover from.... The only dignified course for me would be to go to General Grant and surrender myself and take the consequences of my acts."

That, of course, is what he did. In the most dramatic scene in American history, he surrendered to Grant in the McLean house at Appomattox Courthouse, Virginia, and the Union general accepted the surrender with genuinely magnanimous terms. What would have been the result of Lee's adopting guerrilla warfare instead of surrendering? The New Englander Charles Francis Adams, Jr., an ardent admirer of Lee, said it would have reduced the South to a "smouldering wilderness." The acclaimed Civil War writer Bruce Catton said, "We have had national peace since the war ended... and I think the way Lee and his soldiers conducted themselves in the hours of surrender has a great deal to do with it."

I agree with these conclusions. No doubt, with Lee's blessing the South could have waged a formidable resistance by guerrilla warfare. It would have released the Nathan Bedford Forrests, John Hunt Morgans, John Singleton Mosbys, and Joseph Wheelers to do their violent work. But I concur with Lee that in the end it would have been futile and would have visited indescribable physical, political, economic, and social havoc upon a South already prostrate from four years of war between the armies. It would have inflamed sectional hostilities to a point that a true national reunion, a spiritual reunion, would have been virtually impossible. It would have ignited unquenchable class and racial hatreds within the region and would have turned the South into a cauldron of terrorism. For Lee's decision to surrender with dignity and finality, all Americans owe him an incalculable debt of gratitude.

Lee accepted the outcome of the conflict. Refusing to join fellow Confederates who sought refuge in Brazil, Mexico, and elsewhere, he remained in Virginia. "I cannot desert my native state in the hour of her adversity," he said. "I must abide her fortunes, and share her fate." He advised fellow Southerners to rear their children to be Americans, and to go to work in rebuilding their shattered homes and cities and their economy.

Lee emerged from the Civil War as one of the greatest military commanders of modern times. Many nations would have welcomed his services. Former comrades offered him lucrative business positions; an Englishman offered him an estate and a pension. He rejected these tempting opportunities.

Instead, he set an example for all by following his own advice; he promptly went to work to rebuild Virginia and the

South. He chose to do so through the agency of education, which he wisely believed was the most effective way to accomplish his goal. He said, "I consider the proper education of youth one of the most important objects now to be attained, and one from which the greatest benefits may be expected. Nothing will compensate us for the depression of the standard of our moral and intellectual culture, and each state should take the most energetic measures to revive its schools and colleges, and, if possible, to increase the facilities of instruction and to elevate the standard of living."

Among the observable ways his influence showed itself were the countless Southern children who became his namesakes. A number of my schoolmates in Tennessee bore his name. One of my uncles had the marvelously evocative name Lee Jackson Roland. The practice of paying homage to Lee by bearing his name was not exclusively Southern. One of my army friends in World War II was a descendant of Bohemian immigrants who had settled in Nebraska. His name was Robert Lee Kriz. The full name of the renowned New England poet Robert Frost was Robert Lee Frost.

Keenly aware that his role of command in the war had placed him in a special and awesome relationship with the youth of the South, Lee said, "I have a self-imposed task which I must accomplish. I have seen many of [the young men] fall under my standard. I shall devote all my life now to training young men to do their duty in life." Indeed, he accepted the presidency of the bankrupt Washington College and guided the school to a distinguished position in the realm of higher education.

Intelligence and character—the very attributes that made Lee a great general—made him a great college president and a great private citizen. His intelligence enabled him to improve and expand the curriculum of the school until it became a model of instruction. His character led him to become a monumental influence for good on his students and on great numbers of other Americans in all regions and walks of life.

Lee considered moral training to be Washington College's highest goal. He said on one occasion, "If I could only know that all the young men in the college were good Christians, I should have nothing more to desire." Introducing the honor system of discipline, he told newcomers, "We have but one rule here, and it is that every student must be a gentleman."

Just as he had refused to be bound by tradition in his military thinking, he now refused to be fettered by conventional ideas on education. While he did not desert the classics or cultural studies, he broadened the school's curriculum so as to provide practical and professional training, adding schools of engineering and law along with courses in agriculture, commerce, applied chemistry, journalism, history, and modern languages. Lee contemplated adding a medical school when sufficient funds were available. In the words of his famed biographer Douglas Southall Freeman, "Defeated in war, Lee triumphed in his labor to upbuild the South."

Lee was a great American hero who was doomed to defeat by a fatal cleft in his sense of loyalty. His rise out of the ashes of defeat is one of the miracles of our history. I would close these remarks by repeating, with emphasis, Sir Winston Churchill's one-sentence eulogy of the man we are here to honor. Churchill said, "Lee was one of the noblest Americans who ever lived, and one of the greatest captains known to the annals of war."

Charles P. Roland is Emeritus Alumni Professor of History at the University of Kentucky.

Thomas Lee, Robert E. Lee's great-great uncle,

built his house at Stratford, Virginia, to reflect his political

and social status. Thomas was a senior member of

the Council of Virginia and was its president at the time

of his death in 1750. In 1807 Robert E. Lee was the last male

Lee to be born at Stratford. After the Lees sold the house in 1822,

it was in private hands for over a century. The property

was purchased in 1929 by the Robert E. Lee Memorial

Foundation [now Association] to be restored

and opened to the public.

NON INCAUTUS FUTURI

Philip Ludwell Lee Esqr.
of the Inner Temple LONDON.

The coat-of-arms, borne by the Lee family of

Coton Hall in England, was used by the early generations

of Lees in America who were descended from Richard Lee.

Some versions, such as this one from Philip Ludwell Lee's

bookplate, show the Coton Lee arms quartered with

the Astley arms, which were a pierced five-leaved figure within

a scalloped ermine border on a blue field.

The motto accompanying the arms varies in different

branches of the family, but the Lees in Virginia often used

the motto Non Incautus Futuri *which means*

"not unmindful of the future."